PRESENTED TO:

_____

FROM:

_____

DATE:

_____

HOPE
for a

Kathy Troccoli

Woman's Heart

J Countryman

NASHVILLE, TENNESSEE
www.jcountryman.com

Published by J. Countryman®

a division of Thomas Nelson, Inc., Nashville, Tennessee 37214

Unless otherwise noted, all Scripture quotations are from the New King James Version® of the Bible. Copyright © Thomas Nelson.

The New International Version of the Bible (NIV) © 1984 by the International Bible Society. Used by permission of Zondervan Bible Publishers.

"Break My Heart" Words by Kathy Troccoli

Copyright © 2000 Sony/ATV Songs LLC. All rights on behalf of Sony/ATV.

Songs LLC administered by Sony/ATV Music Publishing, 8 Music Square West, Nashville, TN 37203. All rights reserved. Used by permission.

Project Editor: Pat Matuszak

Design: Christopher Gilbert, UDG | DesignWorks, Sisters, Oregon

ISBN 0-8499-55319

Printed and bound in USA

I waited patiently for the LORD;
he turned to me and heard my cry.
He lifted me out of the slimy pit,
out of the mud and mire;
he set my feet on a rock
and gave me a firm place to stand.
He put a new song in my mouth,
a hymn of praise to our God.
Many will see and fear
and put their trust in the LORD.

PSALM 40:1-3 (NIV)

GOD *of all* *Hope*

Sometimes life's storms catch us unaware. We get caught without an umbrella as torrents of difficulty start to fall.

Other times we hear a distant thunder. An uneasy restlessness in the atmosphere. We sense a storm brewing that is about to burst out upon our quiet world . . .

Every single day, life unfolds—revealing terrible tragedies along with sheer joys . . . carrying every emotion and circumstance imaginable or unimaginable. Life's slow unfolding stops for no one.

Sometimes the fists are raised toward heaven, sometimes the tears flow like a gushing river, sometimes those tears are held back by a dam of anger—and sometimes, knees fall to the ground as a soul abandons everything to the One in control of it all.

WE QUESTION

How many times do you think Almighty God has heard…

> *Why is this happening?*
> *How could You allow this?*
> *If You were a loving God, You would do things differently.*
> *That person doesn't deserve this!*
> *God, where are You?*

These questions have been ringing in God's ears from the Garden of Eden all the way into the twenty-first century. We don't understand His ways, we question His wisdom, we wrestle with our faith, and ultimately, we wonder:

JUST HOW MUCH CAN I TRUST GOD?

SOMETIMES *God's* ANSWER *is a* QUESTION

I love the fact that God has wanted to communicate intimately with us since the beginning of creation. He has chosen His words carefully and has used them in so many different ways.

With them, He has often instructed us, comforted us, rebuked us, and convicted us. I know that in my own life nothing has pierced the very core of me like the Word of God. There are times when I have been so bound in the cords of anger, and then I'll read a couple of His words and feel my heart melt like ice under hot water. I have been so broken and so heartsick, then I've read a psalm or heard a song about Him and a supernatural hope has mended my wounds. But God doesn't necessarily give us an answer during our trials—sometimes He asks us a question. Amidst all of our anger. Amidst all of our doubts. Amidst all of our sadness and our questions. He asks a question back:

"AM I NOT STILL GOD?"

OUR TEARS DO NOT *fall* WITHOUT
THE HAND OF *God* CATCHING
EVERY ONE

His *Ears* Are Listening *to our* Cry

*T*he Lord gently invades those places in us that we have endeavored to protect with neat little walls.

You desire truth in the inward parts, and in the hidden part You will make me to know wisdom.

PSALM 51:6

He teaches us, not just to let us see ourselves correctly, but to help us see Him correctly. I believe that's why so many times in the Scripture He asks a question. There are so many other ways He can approach us, and yet He chooses to ask questions. These questions began at the very beginning.

"WHERE *are* YOU?"

Those three words represent so much. When God called out to Adam and Eve, He was after something. He desired something. Something way beyond what He was asking.

What God desired was honesty. He wanted Adam and Eve to answer Him with the truth. He desired for His children to realize where they were. Tell Him where they were. That would be their first step in realizing the state of their hearts and their desperate need for Him.

I have learned that the Lord is always on a pursuit to get to the heart of the matter.

"Come now, and let us reason together,"
says the LORD.
"Though your sins are like scarlet,
they shall be as white as snow..."

ISAIAH 1:18

We keep changing the bandages instead of running to God and saying, "Heal me, Lord—whatever it takes." We hide and we keep on hiding. Like Adam and Eve, God speaks to us: "Why are you doing that? I see it all." He wants us to come to Him with abandon.

KISSED *by the* *King*

I often talk about "being kissed by the King." It's my way to describe those amazing, intimate moments when we sense God's presence in a tangible way. He kisses away our tears, our heartache.

Oh, how I love this psalm:

> *The eyes of the LORD are on the righteous,*
> *and His ears are open to their cry. ...*
> *The righteous cry out, and the LORD hears,*
> *and delivers them out of all their troubles.*
> *The LORD is near to those who have a broken heart,*
> *and saves such as have a contrite spirit.*
> *Many are the afflictions of the righteous,*
> *but the LORD delivers him out of them all.*

> PSALM 34:15, 17-19

Though these words have ministered to countless believers over the ages, when I read them in the midst of all my pain, I feel that the angel of the Lord is encamping around me, that the Lord is tenderly speaking to me.

GOD *Gives* US
GLIMPSES OF *Heaven*

Splashes of the beyond.

Hints—

of the real world

the unseen world.

What joy to know that eternal life awaits us—

Jesus is our hope.

THE *Father's* CALL

*S*ometimes God uses people to teach us what His heart is like. My earthly father taught me a love for people, and I pray I'm giving him the honor of being a woman who yearns to have the heart of God. When I first started singing, my dad would knock on my bedroom door and say,

"Please sing for me. Sing for Daddy."

I would oftentimes be annoyed at the interruption or would say something like,

"Not now, Dad. I don't feel like it."

He would reply like a child,

"Come on. Just a little bit. Just one song."

Boy … do I wish I had serenaded him more. Each time my voice rises toward heaven, I hope my dad gets to hear the song.

"HE WILL *Rejoice* OVER YOU WITH SINGING … "

ZEPHANIAH 3:17

JESUS *sees us* THROUGH ADORING EYES.

*H*e sees us cleansed in Him. And He sees our potential. We are the Shulamite maiden, and we are as lovely in His eyes as Cinderella was to the prince. She, too, had trouble believing her loveliness. She fled at midnight, thinking her loveliness lay in her appearance. But her prince pursued her, just as our Prince pursues us. He is on a quest for our love. And yes, He will still love us tomorrow.

Many waters cannot quench love,

Nor can the floods drown it.

SONG OF SOLOMON 8:7

First LOVE

y "once upon a time" with God began on August 5, 1978, when I prayed that Jesus would come and live inside my heart. The fact that this God whom I'd seen every Sunday hanging on the cross could be known intimately overwhelmed me. This was all such a revelation to me.

That day I felt like a bride, a princess. The perfect man had found me. I was face-to-face with perfect love and promises that wouldn't be broken. I knew in my spirit that His hand would never let go of mine and that He had just been waiting for my "Yes."

"I HAVE LOVED YOU WITH AN EVERLASTING LOVE;
I HAVE DRAWN YOU WITH LOVING KINDNESS."

JEREMIAH 31:3 (NIV)

"GOD IS LOVE. WHOEVER *Lives* IN LOVE LIVES IN *God,* AND GOD IN HIM."

1 JOHN 4:16

AT THE *Heart* OF LOVE

*W*hat else do we really need to know in this life if we can know the very heart of God? Not only has He ordained us to communicate with Him intimately, but He truly desires to reveal His heart and His will to us. We journey through this mortal life as if we have a "seasonal" relationship with God. "I felt close to Him last summer but I'm feeling real far away from Him this spring." We go in and out like the tide. Today I believe Him, but tomorrow I may not. Who has left? Not God. He always stays. That's what I love about Him. Why do we easily forget about the gift we have in Jesus? A true confidante. A safe keeper of our secrets. A lover of our souls. There is an abundance of eternal treasure waiting to be discovered. There will always be mystery to God until we see Him face to face—but there is so much we could experience here and now. He longs to give us His jewels. Whether they are coming out of His mouth or displayed in the fabric of our lives, God Almighty wants to lavish us with all that He is. He always wants to let us know He loves us. And He will always find a way.

Choose life, that both you and your descendants may live;

and that you may love the LORD your

God, that you may obey His voice,

and that you may cling to Him, for He is your life…

DEUTERONOMY 30:19-20

Choosing life. Holding fast to Him. It is our decision. God will never force Himself and His will on anyone. He will let us decide.

When I said,

"Yes Lord"!

a major stake was put in the ground. My tent was pitched in God's camp. It was the beginning of my being protected from bitterness.

Talk TO JESUS

*H*e doesn't need an abundance of words. He doesn't need a dissertation about your life. He just wants your attention. He wants your heart. Feel far away from Him? Move closer. Feel close? Move closer still.

> *Draw near to God and*
>
> *He will draw near to you.*
>
> JAMES 4 : 8

PROMISE OF HOPE

One thing is for certain. We have a promise for our future. This we learn through the book of Job:

"BUT HE KNOWS THE *Way* THAT I TAKE;
BUT HE HAS *Tested* ME,
I SHALL COME FORTH AS GOLD"

JOB 23:10

We must not "forget to remember." We must remind ourselves of what the Lord has done and what He will continue to do according to His promises.

THE ONE WHO

"THE SPIRIT OF THE *Lord* GOD IS UPON ME,
BECAUSE THE LORD HAS ANOINTED *Me* TO PREACH
GOOD TIDINGS TO THE POOR; HE HAS SENT ME TO HEAL
THE BROKENHEARTED, TO PROCLAIM LIBERTY
TO THE CAPTIVES..."

ISAIAH 61:1

is our *Hope*

"Come!"

The invitation is always open to commune with God. No matter what. And the funny thing is that when we move an inch He'll move a mile. In those desperate times when we feel like we don't have an ounce of strength to "come," He will gently pick up our heads so that our eyes can behold some-thing—something that will keep His hope alive in us. We are never without a source of hope. He will always come. Jesus will reach for you in ways that will break your heart. And if your heart cannot grasp it at the time—He will gently remind you of it later.

"Come to Me, all you who labor and are heavy laden, and I will give you rest. Take my yoke upon you and learn from Me, for I am gentle and lowly in heart, and you will find rest for your souls. For My yoke is easy and My burden is light."

MATTHEW 11:28-30

POURING *in the* LIFE
OF CHRIST

I have learned that if I don't give access to the truths of God to enter my heart, many other "voices" will get my attention. Especially in times of crisis. We are so vulnerable. We can easily despair and feel hopeless. Our emotions are tossed back and forth like ping-pong balls. One day we're "fine." The next day we're "losing it." Even when we don't have the strength to read, or to put "good" things into our souls, we must somehow allow words of life to be spoken over our loved ones and ourselves. Obviously, the source of life is Scripture, but words of love could also come from a lovely book, a sweet card, or an encouraging letter. A prayer from a fellow believer could also be what blows a breath of life into our deflated hearts. The Lord comes in so many wondrous and miraculous ways. It's just that He doesn't always come in ways we expect.

Love Is Waiting

It always amazes me how Jesus is constantly aware of the state of our hearts. He doesn't miss a thing. We get bogged down with all sorts of duties that "just need to get done." We are concerned about how we look, and we spend a great deal of time on "our complete package." We worry about what success looks like and take pride in how others perceive us. We are consumed with all sorts of things.

And all the while Jesus waits.

If we are not consumed with God, we will most definitely be consumed with other things. We were created to worship God and if we don't set our affections there, we will easily worship something or someone else.

SET YOUR MINDS ON THINGS *above*

NOT ON *Earthly* THINGS.

COLOSSIANS 3:2 (NIV)

Out *of the* Box

*J*esus is unconventional. He'll work in ways you may not recognize or understand. And He is big enough to do the things you have labeled impossible.

He has enough power.

He has enough time.

He is bigger than your problem.

Believe in Him more than in what you may see. Trust in Him more than what you may feel. You can question. He can handle your questions. God is highly confident of His own plans. He can do everything but fail.

ETERNAL PERSPECTIVE

*W*e all have trouble seeing as God does because He looks through binoculars and we look through pinholes. He stands right next to us and says, "I see, I see. I know, I know."

And, as we squint through our pinholes in frustration, we refuse to accept His comfort.

At the end of the whole picture, God always has the same goal. The goal is the glory of His Son, Jesus Christ. He wants Him high and lifted up. We want immediate answers. He loves us too much to bring a fleeting gratification to our hearts that may cause a momentary happiness.

His concern is the eternal well-being of our lives. There is always a much higher goal. What we don't understand is that when Jesus is ultimately glorified, our souls will be at peace and filled with an unspeakable joy because we were created to glorify Jesus. We weren't created to "have our way" and "live our way." We were created to worship God and trust Him with His way. That is where abundant life of the soul will be discovered and lived out.

FOR WITH *God* NOTHING WILL BE IMPOSSIBLE.

LUKE 1:37

*T*wo of the most significant words about the tender heart of Christ are:

"Jesus Wept"

I suppose He cried for many different reasons. He cried because He was human. He cried because of His love for Lazarus and for the pain of His friends. He cried because of His disappointment with the things of this world. His intention was to give us heaven.

The Lord is extremely sensitive to tears. When you think about the fact that He created our bodies, doesn't it just blow your mind that He gave us tear ducts? We didn't have to be put together in a way that crying was an option. Yet He gave us these little tiny holes for all that water to flow through. It is His brilliant way for us to dispose of our pain. He knew we would laugh until we cried and we would grieve with a wrenching far too deep for words.

Our eyes are the windows to our souls, and it is only natural for them to release the truth of what is being felt there. God knew life would be filled with moments of joy but also be laden with sorrow. When He was here in the flesh, He experienced all of life and all of the emotions we experience. He had feelings like us and He cried like us and with us. But someday He will wipe away our tears.

JESUS LIVED AND HE STILL *Lives*.
OUR *Real* SAVIOR
OUR REAL LORD.
THE MAKER OF *History* WILL BE THE
SUMMATION OF HISTORY.

TEARS *in a* BOTTLE

You number my wanderings;

Put my tears into Your bottle;

Are they not in Your book?

PSALM 56:8

*J*esus holds my tears in a bottle. Our tears. Not one of them falls to the ground without His hands intervening to save them.

He knew we would desperately be in need of hope. And He knew He would be that hope in our suffering. The cross would bring about resurrection for Him and for all who would choose to believe in Him.

Jesus will *Never* Forget *our* Tears

Haven't we often thought we were alone in our grief? That God has forgotten us? "He's God and He can do something!" we cry. Meanwhile, He is always "doing something." Even when He is seemingly doing nothing, He is doing something. A behind-the-scenes Director who is orchestrating a Divine story. There is always a purpose. Always a plan. There is always the glory of God at hand, and His will most definitely will be accomplished. He feels deeply. He is moved greatly. He lets us bury our heads in His chest, and as He wipes our tears He wipes His own.

Do *You* Believe *This?*

*I*n John 11:25, Jesus said to Martha, "I am the resurrection and the life. He who believes in me will live, even though he dies; and whoever lives and believes in me will never die."

Then He asked her a question:

"Do you believe this?"

"Yes, Lord," she told him, "I believe that you are the Christ, the Son of God, who was to come into the world."

We can answer the Lord today. And when He asks again tomorrow, we can answer Him again. Our response will affect not only ourselves but those around us. Will we become embittered or empowered?

Our decision doesn't affect whether He is or isn't. But He most certainly wants to hear our answer. He takes great delight in our trust.

PSALM OF HOPE

Those who sat in darkness and in the shadow of death,

Bound in affliction and irons . . .

They fell down, and there was none to help.

Then they cried out to the LORD in their trouble,

And He saved them out of their distresses.

He brought them out of the darkness and the shadow of death,

And broke their chains in pieces.

PSALM 107: 10-14

The One Who is
Our *Hope*

*P*salm 107 lists many of the prisons from which God has
set us free. It is a psalm of hope, a psalm that gives us
encouragement that no matter how deep our pit, God can free
us. The key, whether we are in a maximum-security prison, a
prison of our own making, or a prison that was built around us,
is to thirst for the Living God. He is the One who is our hope.
He is the One who holds the key to unlock our chains.

SPEAKING *to your* SOUL

*E*very single one of us, even after we know Jesus, will have times of discouragement, depression, and even despair. David, who had a heart for God, frequently had times like that. What did he do? He talked to his soul, reminding his soul of the reasons it could hope in God.

Why are you downcast, O my soul?
Why so disturbed within me?
Put your hope in God,
for I will yet praise Him,
my Savior and my God.

PSALM 42:11 (NIV)

FREEDOM *for the* Captive

I don't know what it feels like to be locked up behind bars.
I don't know what it feels like to wake up and not
be able to do whatever I'd like to do.

But let me tell you something…

I do know what it's like to wake up in the
morning with that all-too-familiar excruciating
pain in my gut at the realization that I have to
face another day feeling my own heartbeat.

I do know what it's like to question
God and beat my fists against heaven until
I've exhausted my last ounce of
strength.

I do know what it's like to feel
utterly hopeless.

That is when I am so thankful
that He continues to rub His
liniment of love on a heart that
can be so bruised—fighting to
heal its own wounds.

God's *Eye*

I can never live without the light of Jesus. I've got to keep my heart in the light. When I sense the darkness, I must remember that the darkness is not dark to God. He sees what we cannot.

FOR YOU WERE ONCE DARKNESS, BUT NOW YOU ARE
LIGHT IN THE LORD. WALK AS CHILDREN OF LIGHT
(FOR THE FRUIT OF THE SPIRIT IS IN ALL GOODNESS,
RIGHTEOUSNESS, AND TRUTH), FINDING OUT WHAT IS
ACCEPTABLE TO THE LORD. AND HAVE NO FELLOWSHIP
WITH THE UNFRUITFUL WORKS OF DARKNESS, BUT
RATHER EXPOSE THEM.

Ephesians 5:8-11

No Hiding Out

*I*t is crucial not to isolate ourselves in times of despair. The typical response to despair is to want to hide in the dark, to stay under the covers. But isolation just sends us further down the spiral, deeper into the pit. We are not allowing anything to come and buffet us up to the truth. We can't recognize lies until we know the truth. I know that in my own life, when I'm in that state and Sunday morning comes, I don't want to get up out of bed. I cheat my spirit of the very water for which it is so parched. Or, the phone rings and my immediate heart response is: "I don't want to see anybody. I don't want to talk to anybody." Those are the very times when we need to remain open. There are people we know who can speak "life" to us, and we must allow them to have access to us. We need to be willing not to wallow in the comforting bed of self-pity.

WORDS *of* COMFORT

from the $\mathcal{L}ord$

BOUNDLESS LOVE

*T*here is nothing, absolutely nothing that God will not forgive. You cannot "out-sin" His forgiveness. You cannot "out-sin" the love of God. You must know that it is the heart of God to set the captive free. We are all held captive by so many different things. Jesus can search out the deepest, darkest places in us.

IF WE CONFESS OUR SINS, HE IS
Faithful AND JUST AND WILL FORGIVE US
OUR SINS AND *purify* US FROM
ALL UNRIGHTEOUSNESS

1 JOHN 1:9 (NIV)

For I am persuaded that neither death nor life, nor angels nor principalities nor powers, nor things present nor things to come, nor height nor depth, nor any other created thing, shall be able to separate us from the love of God which is in Christ Jesus our Lord.

ROMANS 8:38

GRACE THAT IS GREATER

Not one of us is exempt from restoration or the joy of having a redeemed heart. It does take courage. It does take persistence. It does take a "wanting" for the higher things of God and a commitment to take the higher road to get there. The grace of God will always be there waiting with outstretched arms.

He will give you the grace to change. He will give you the grace to be set free. He will give you the grace to believe Him.

HEBREWS 12:15 (NIV) SAYS:

See to it that no one misses the grace of God.

By the grace and mercy of God, I will truly work out my salvation with fear and trembling.

> *Show me Your ways, O LORD;*
> *Teach me Your paths.*
> *Lead me in Your truth and teach me,*
> *For You are the God of my salvation;*
> *On You I wait all the day.*
> *Remember, O LORD, Your tender mercies and Your*
> *lovingkindnesses . . .*
> *According to your mercy remember me,*
> *For Your goodness' sake, O LORD.*

PSALM 25:4-7

WORDS OF *Life*

*M*usic with lyrics of praise and worship to God Almighty and Scripture are medicine to every cell of my soul. They revive me. Healing words spoken over me are like a flashlight in a dark closet. We have no idea of the power of words and their effect on our spiritual and emotional well-being.

The tongue has the power of life and death . . .

PROVERBS 18:21 (NIV)

WE ARE *Miracles* IN THE MAKING

IF WE WANT TO BE. IT'S OUR CHOICE.

GIVE THANKS *to the* *Lord* FOR *His* UNFAILING LOVE.

*M*any times I bow beneath the cross of Christ. We are all mendable. We are all healable. We are all restorable. He will set us free. Believe that He can heal you.

"...GIVE THEM BEAUTY FOR ASHES,

THE OIL OF JOY FOR MOURNING,

THE GARMENT OF PRAISE FOR THE SPIRIT

OF HEAVINESS;

THAT THEY MAY BE CALLED TREES OF RIGHTEOUSNESS,

THE PLANTING OF THE LORD, THAT HE

MAY BE GLORIFIED."

Isaiah 61:3

PUT YOUR *Hope* IN *God*

We have to keep in the light. Once again, I know that in my own life I need to stay in the light. I won't experience the truth, the warmth, and the health of the Lord's light if I stay in and around the dark.

It's a process. And it's a sacred journey with you and the Lord. And we must be daily aware of living the life of Jesus. Let's continually fill ourselves up to the brim with "good" things.

DISPLAYING
THE *Heart* OF GOD

A great Scottish preacher said: The most profane word we use is "hopeless." When you say a situation or a person is hopeless, you are slamming the door in the face of God.

Don't slam the door in the face of the One who offers you hope. Your circumstances are part of a much bigger plan.

ONE DAY WE
WILL SEE...

*W*hen we are with the Lord, we will understand
everything, because we will be face to face with Him.
Now, Paul tells us, we "see but a poor reflection as in a mirror."
We only know in part. So life will often confuse us, often make
us feel frustrated. Often our soul will be downcast.

When King David was talking to his soul in Psalm 42, there
were times when he seemed to be sinking, when waves of
despair crashed over him and he cried out to God.

WHY ARE YOU CAST DOWN, O MY *Soul?*

AND WHY ARE YOU DISQUIETED WITHIN ME?

HOPE IN *God*, FOR I SHALL YET PRAISE HIM

FOR THE HELP OF *His* COUNTENANCE.

O MY GOD, MY SOUL IS CAST DOWN WITHIN ME;

THEREFORE I WILL *Remember* YOU...

PSALM 42: 5-6

Psalm 91

This became my mother's favorite psalm. The whole picture it portrays—of being in the shadow of the Almighty—is what I saw my mom doing. You have to be very close to someone to sit in their shadow. The closer Mom came to leaving this earth, the closer she drew to God. She was sitting in His shadow. Though her pain continued, God was with her:

He who dwells in the secret place of the Most High

Shall abide under the shadow of the Almighty.

I will say of the LORD, "He is my refuge and my fortress;

My God, in Him I will trust."

Surely He shall deliver you from the snare of the fowler

And from the perilous pestilence.

He shall cover you with His feathers,

And under His wings you shall take refuge;

His truth shall be your shield and buckler.

You shall not be afraid of the terror by night . . .

For He shall give His angels charge over you

to keep you in all your ways . . .

"Because he has set his love upon Me,

therefore I will deliver him;

I will set him on high, because he has known My name.

He shall call upon Me, and I will answer him;

I will be with him in trouble;

I will deliver him and honor him."

PSALM 91:1-15

SURELY GOODNESS
AND *Mercy*

*Y*ou can anchor yourself to faith like a stake in the ground today. Wrap your hands tightly around it and claim what is yours in Jesus Christ. His truth is ours to build our lives on. His life is ours to cling to. The hope of Him is our survival. His love is what will carry us and sustain us.

THE LORD WILL ACCOMPLISH WHAT CONCERNS ME.

PSALM 138:8 (NASB)

THE LORD IS CLOSE TO THE BROKENHEARTED
AND SAVES THOSE WHO ARE CRUSHED IN SPIRIT.

PSALM 34:18 (NIV)

WEEPING MAY REMAIN FOR A NIGHT, BUT REJOICING
COMES IN THE MORNING.

PSALM 30:5 (NIV)

BEYOND *Happiness*

$\mathscr{T}$he happiness we desire so desperately in this life may not be what God wants to give us to "fill" our souls. He sees way beyond our circumstances. He can and will deliver a supernatural contentment and peace that is not dependent upon anything we may go through in this life.

Oswald Chambers said:

"It is not our circumstances, but God in our circumstances."

He wants to fill our souls with Himself. With His life. Happiness dries up. Eternal joy abounds forever. That gift is only found in Him.

That's Jesus. He is our hope.

And, by the way, we do have a happily ever after. He promises it.

ROLLER COASTER HOPE

*W*ithout knowing God and knowing who we are in Him, we will constantly take our faith on a roller-coaster ride. It will go up and it will go down. We'll scream at the treacherous turns and close our eyes when we start speeding into a steep downward spiral. Trust doesn't change God, but it will certainly change the ride. Putting your complete confidence in Jesus does change the quality of your life. It affects your peace and it affects your joy.

PLANTING *Hope*

*T*rust makes you able to endure circumstances that seem humanly unbearable. Watchman Nee said:

"To hold on to the plough, while wiping our tears—this is Christianity."

Every day either He is God or He is not. How do we make that choice? What gives us the power to pick Jesus? It is knowing Him and knowing who we are in Him.

Comfort

When there seem to be no answers there may seem to be no God. We'll think, "He hasn't exactly come through like I thought He would, so I really question His other promises." All of us have gone through different seasons of this at different times in our lives. I love what C. S. Lewis said:

"It is quite useless knocking at the door of heaven for earthly comfort. It's not the sort of comfort they supply there."

BEYOND OUR VISION

Often God doesn't give us answers to our questions, but instead He questions us. God is mysterious. He is also mercy and love. We must live in the balance of that fact. He is bigger than we are. He is wiser than we are. We'll acknowledge that on most "good" days, but when the hard days come we can question His very existence. We must remember that we have "blind spots" and God doesn't. He sees up close and at the very same time looks way beyond what we can see.

I Know *Whom* I Have Believed

*A*s someone once said, we can't change the wind, but we can adjust our sails. How do we adjust our sails? By remembering what we know about Him.

We must be certain of who He is. We must be certain of His character.

When things happen in our lives that don't make sense and others want to accuse God of wrongdoing, we have to rest on the character of God and His history of faithfulness. God may not explain. He may not reveal His plan. But He has revealed Himself. Everything we question about the hardships of life, its injustices and its tragedies, should be processed through what we know about Jesus Christ.

In this is love, not that we loved God, but that He loved us and sent His Son to be the propitiation for our sins.

1 JOHN 4:10

WE LOVE HIM *Because* HE FIRST LOVED US.

1 JOHN 4:19

Friends who
Hope with us

I have had the blessing of having incredible friends in my life. They have provided for me, cared for me, and comforted me. They have prayed for me and loved me in ways I will be thankful for far into eternity. Many times I have seen first hand that love "believes the best." I have also seen how love "covers" and protects.

Love . . . always protects, always trusts, always hopes,
always perseveres.

I Corinthians 13 : 6 - 7 (NIV)

GOD'S PLAN

Based on our knowing God and His character, we can say, with confidence:

God has a plan for my future that is good and not evil.

God will never leave me or forsake me.

God loves me with an undying love. It is penetrating, persevering and stubborn.

God is faithful to forgive my sins.

God will keep His promises.

THE SCRIPTURES SAY IN 2 PETER 3:18:

"...GROW IN THE GRACE AND KNOWLEDGE OF OUR LORD AND SAVIOR JESUS CHRIST."

WHO *do you* THINK YOU *Are?*

*Y*ou must always remember who you are to Jesus. Remind yourself every day who you are in Him. It will give you a holy confidence. Thelma Wells has said that God has one weakness: He has a weak spot for us.

REMEMBER TO TELL YOURSELF:

> *I am His child.*
>
> *I belong to Him.*
>
> *I am His Beloved.*
>
> *I am a conqueror.*
>
> *I am precious in His sight.*
>
> *Know who you are.*

LEAVE LITTLE ROOM FOR DOUBT.

Make a way for hope.

KNOW THE ONE WHO IS LORD.

A KINGDOM *of* HOPE

*J*esus was the epitome of "knowing who He was." Picture this: At the Last Supper, while the disciples were arguing about who was going to be the greatest in the kingdom of heaven, what was Jesus doing? He was washing their feet! How could He do this? He knew who He was. He knew why He came. He knew His Father was sufficient to meet His deepest needs.

We all have a craving for affirmation. It's only human. We were created with all kinds of "soul" needs. Jesus is the only One who can meet them all.

Man hides his own things
in order to conceal them;
God hides His own things
in order to reveal them.

SECRET *Hope*

In Matthew 6:6, Jesus says:

"...when you pray, go into your room, close the door and pray to your Father, who is unseen. Then your Father, who sees what is done in secret, will reward you." (NIV)

There are two key words here. *Unseen* and *secret*. This is what Jesus asks us to do. Pray to our Father who is unseen, who sees what is done in secret. These words are mentioned clearly. Jesus works through and in the unseen and the secret. Sometimes we wish He would hold a press conference and explain what He is doing. We want to understand clearly and know immediately. It is just in our nature. But it is not in His nature to do so. Look at how He handled His own deity. He didn't walk around with a sign on His back that said,

I AM THE SON OF GOD!

He just was. He just is.

KEEPER *of our* SECRETS

*J*esus lived on this earth and He can live in our hearts.
Unseen but known. Knowing secrets but holding them
close to His heart. He knows what we can handle. He knows the
right time for "revelation." We have to trust Him to hold the
answers until He decides to boldly display them before our eyes.

Heroes of Hope

*E*ach one of us is encouraged when we look at the lives of those who have sailed on successfully and victoriously, even in the most treacherous of waters. People who have been up against spiritual tidal waves and hurricanes. Their needs were great and they met them with Jesus.

If we are honest, we'll admit that so often we walk around with a cup in our hands saying, "Is there anyone out there who can fill my cup?" All the while Jesus is waiting for us to find our fulfillment in Him. Everything else should be the overflow.

HEALING WOUNDS

*T*he Bible says that the Spirit that raised Christ from the dead lives in us. What a testimony to the fact that God will give His Spirit without boundaries to anyone who allows Him freedom to do so.

I find comfort in the testimonies I hear. They build my faith. They strengthen my courage. Many times when we see each other's wounds we are comforted. They are a witness of the grace of God. They are a confirmation that His promises are true.

We shouldn't ever keep God's love to ourselves. It gives. It suffers with. It must be demonstrated.

Suffering

As long as we are under this great big sky there will be suffering. But rest assured that when you suffer as a Christian your suffering is not in vain.

To bestow on them a crown of beauty instead of ashes, the oil of gladness, instead of mourning, and a garment of praise instead of a spirit of despair. . .

ISAIAH 61:3 (NIV)

FOR OUR LIGHT AND MOMENTARY *Troubles* ARE
ACHIEVING FOR US AN *Eternal* GLORY THAT
FAR OUTWEIGHS THEM ALL.

2 CORINTHIANS 4:17 (NIV)

THE *Life* INSIDE

*T*ake a picture of a healthy tree in the prime season of summer. The brilliance of the colors can be breathtaking. There is vibrancy. There is growth. There is life. Look at the same tree in the height of fall. Empty. Stripped. Alive on the inside, but dead on the outside.

How true it is for us as God's children. In this life our flesh may be dying, our circumstances may leave us feeling stripped of our pride or dignity, and our lives may seem empty of any promise. But the Spirit that raised Jesus from the dead lives inside of us! We are never without the life of God. We are never without hope. It is always within our grasp. We are never without the certainty of His promises. They are always there for us to build our lives upon.

For we know that if our earthly house,

this tent, is destroyed, we have a building from God, a house

not made with hands, eternal in the heavens.

2 CORINTHIANS 5:1

GOD *who is* THERE

The Lord wants to teach me many things about myself and many things about Him. He cares about my future and He cares about my dreams. He is far more concerned with the condition of my heart than the circumstances that I see around me.

I must tell you that times of doubt and discouragement have all been used to allow me to receive God's best. They have been used to continue to get me to "look up." They have been used to let me know that my self-worth is found only in Him and in nothing else. They have been used to allow His dreams for me to truly become the dreams I would have for myself.

GOD'S PRIORITIES

God wants His concerns to be my concerns. He wants His priorities to be my priorities.

Let God have His way. Give it all to Him. You will be amazed one day when He rolls the stone away from the tomb of your agendas. You will see it empty. It held your plans, your perspective, and your wisdom. He will then allow you to live into a glorious resurrection. You will fulfill His purpose.

If I rise on the wings of the dawn,
if I settle on the far side of the sea,
even there Your hand will guide me,
Your right hand will hold me fast.
If I say, "Surely the darkness will hide me
and the light become night around me."
even the darkness will not be dark to You.

PSALM 139:9-12 (NIV)

GOD'S GUIDANCE

"Do not let your hearts be troubled. Trust in God; trust also in Me."

JOHN 14:1 (NIV)

In Our Lives

Now He who has prepared us for this very thing is God,

who also has given us the Spirit as a guarantee.

So we are always confident, knowing that while

we are at home in the body we are absent from the Lord.

For we walk by faith, not by sight.

We are confident . . . we make it our aim . . .

to be well pleasing to Him.

2 CORINTHIANS 5:5-9

If We *Share* in His Sufferings...

"Now if we are children, then we are heirs—heirs of God and co-heirs with Christ, if indeed we share in his sufferings in order that we may also share in his glory."

Romans 8:17 (NIV)

Even in the most raging waters, our Lord's hand will guide us and will hold us fast. Even in our darkest moments, the Lord is illuminating and clear. We often wonder, "Do You know what You're doing?" Yes, He does. We can be sure of it. God speaks to us often and says,

"Let Me worry about that."

God's Plans for Us

The Bible says continually that God knows the plans He has for us, and they are for our good. Jesus will always come between us and our sorrow, between us and our fear, between us and our pain. We cannot get away from God. If you read of His presence in Psalm 139, you'll see that it is revelatory!

When we feel like we are spinning out of control
He has hemmed us in—behind and before (vs. 5)
When we're restless and we can't sleep
He knows when we sit and when we rise (vs. 2)
In times of elation and joy
If we go to the heavens, He is there (vs. 8)
In times of depression and despair
If we make our bed in the depths, He is there (vs. 8)
When we experience peace and fulfillment
If we rise on the wings of the dawn, He is there (vs. 9)
When we are uprooted
If we settle on the far side of the sea, He is there (vs. 9)

HOPE *Extraordinary*

Our precious Jesus will meet extraordinary pain with extraordinary grace. He will meet extraordinary needs with extraordinary resources. He will meet extraordinary fears with extraordinary comfort. And although the Lord does care about our deepest needs and is concerned with the details of our lives, He is always on a quest for our hearts. Our faith is what interests Him. It isn't our circumstances. It's the building up of our faith.

GOD'S GOAL

*H*is goal is not necessarily to make us happy.
His goal is to make us His.

There are thousands of times when we'll ask God what He is doing *to* us. We must be more concerned with what He wants to do *in* us. I am talking about conforming us into the image of Christ. And only the Lord knows what it will take to conform us into the image of His son.

John Newton said:

"Trials are medicines which our gracious and wise physician prescribes because we need them; and He proportions the frequency and weight of them to what the case requires. Let us trust in His skill and thank Him for His prescription."

SURRENDERED *in* HOPE

I was amazed when I read a quote from Joni Eareckson Tada. What an unbelievable woman of God. She has been confined to a wheelchair and is one of the most moving speakers I have ever heard. I have had the privilege of doing some conferences with her. I experience the person of Christ in her every time I see her. When I read this quote it didn't surprise me. She said that one of the first things she will say to God in heaven is, "Thanks, I needed that!"

THE HEART *of the* Matter

*G*od is continually after our hearts. Our hearts need to be broken by the things that break the heart of God. Without this work in us we will maneuver ourselves through life with our opinions, our judgments, and our summations. God knows that to build up our faith we need to grow continually in knowledge of Him:

The knowledge of the truth that leads to godliness—a faith and knowledge resting on the hope of eternal life, which God, who does not lie, promised before the beginning of time.

TITUS 1:1-2 (NIV)

This will give us the certainty that He is in control and the security of knowing that His ultimate plan and destination will be accomplished in our lives.

Hope on the High Seas

JESUS SAYS:

"Do not let your hearts be troubled.
Trust in God; trust also in Me." (NIV)

JOHN 14:1

*G*od is the captain of our ship as we sail through storm-tossed seas. His Word is the lighthouse, to protect us from the hidden rocks beneath the dark waters. Ignoring the lighthouse, or "grabbing" the wheel from His capable hands, will lead to destruction. We will surely crash into the rocks and find ourselves sinking.

Often we have no idea where He is taking us. I know I will often look out at the stormy sea and say,

"I'm so glad You know where You're going, because I'm completely lost."

We can trust His heart. We must be on a quest for His heart. That is where the peace will come in. He knows where He wants to take us. He knows what is right for us. Let's let Him get us home without a fight. And He will get us home.

GOD IS FAITHFUL

*P*ain is not an easy topic. The last thing those who are suffering need are pat answers. Tragedies, injustices, and heartaches are not easily explained away, and I'm not convinced they can or should be. What I am convinced about is that we serve a faithful God who has all the answers and is always in control. We don't necessarily need to know the reasons. We just need to know Him. We don't have to give answers to those who are suffering, but we do need to be His love to them.

I Want to *Hold* His Hand

*G*od is so kind. He is so loving and merciful. He does not let go of my hand. He has taught me and continues to teach me His ways. His tender hand has led me to "pleasant places." Nothing in this world can compare to the blessing of the Lord. We experience such joy and fulfillment when we put our trust in Him.

THE PROCESS OF HOPE

*B*ecoming the person God longs for us to be doesn't happen easily or quickly. No one waves a magic wand over your head and—voilà!—the Proverbs 31 woman emerges. It's a process of walking each day with Him. Asking Him to penetrate your soul. Giving Him permission to mold you, change you, shake you, move you. Little by little you will understand:

"HE HAS MADE *Everything* BEAUTIFUL

IN ITS TIME."

ECCLESIASTES 3:11

Trust

*W*hat a big word. Without it we have a pretty superficial relationship with God. Every day we have a choice. Do we trust Him with the hours ahead and with whatever is around the corner? Or do we only want to "lie down in green pastures"?

THERE IS HOPE *In Mercy*

*E*very day we are at the mercy of Jesus. Every day we choose to believe or not to believe. There must be some sort of foundation to build our beliefs upon in order to move forward in our faith. There must be some anchor we use to know we will not be moved. There has to be. Without it, every hour and every emotion that passes will toss us like the wind. That anchor must be Jesus.

We so often encounter a people that have no concept of reality or of the truth of the Gospel. They opt for psychics, stones, and candles because there is no cost. Nothing is required of them there. There is no bottom line to their actions or their morals without the absolute truths of God. It is very easy these days to create our own reality and adhere to it. Jesus challenges us to His reality. Without His influences it is easy to live for our own pleasure, to process life with a selfish heart, and to not know the meaning of the word *humility*.

HOPE FOR LOST SHEEP

We are a generation of people in such desperate need of the love of God and the riches of His wisdom. That's why I yearn to be an ambassador for Jesus Christ. I pray that He will continue to use my gifts to break through the walls of lies that have been erected around the hearts of millions of unknowing people. And "truth" will never be complete unless it is viewed against God's truth. God is "most high." There is no one above Him. Yet we create Him in our own image. As He has pierced this heart of mine with His life, I want to be used in a way that will do the same for others. Lost sheep don't come home. They don't know how. We have to go get them. But we must remember that we can't reach others if we don't allow God to reach us.

WEEPING MAY REMAIN FOR A *Night,*
BUT *Rejoicing* COMES IN THE MORNING.

PSALM 30:5 (NIV)

O Lord My *God*, I Called *to you* For Help

*G*od needed to work on the very core of my soul. He needed to get me to the place where I would be content with Him. He yearned for me to be content with whatever He chose to give me. He longed for me to find joy in what He ordained for my life.

All the prayers. The thousands of prayers. The tears. Through two decades of my life. But God had a plan. He always does. He needed to get me to the point in my life where when He said,

"This is the way. Walk ye in it…"

I would hear. I really would want to go. And I would find joy and peace when I got there.

He is so close to the broken-hearted.

He is so near to the weary soul.

He is so present in our suffering.

He never hides His face but offers a hiding place.

Allow yourself to fall.

He's waiting to catch you.

Two different worlds—the mortal
and the divine.
One so dimly lit and one flooded by
heavenly glory.
The veil lifted from one as the other
waits for its turn.
One grieves and the other knows no sorrow and
so we must wait as we live in this world yet by
the mercy of God taste and touch and glimpse
the gift of eternal life.

WOMAN, *What* DO YOU SEEK?

I want to be faithful to Jesus more than I want to be "successful." I want to crave His voice more than the applause of a crowd. I want to hear, "Well done, my good and faithful servant" when I see Him face to face. That is the award I seek. I want that more than any other reward this life can offer me. Jesus alone. That is my reward.

I want to set my affections on Him. I want to be a holy woman and not just a Christian woman. I know that I don't have anything to offer anyone apart from the life of God in me.

REJOICING
COMES *in the* MORNING

I am seeing more clearly these days. My eyesight is getting worse, but my spiritual sight is getting better. It all makes a little more sense to me now. I don't always have to "understand" to have His peace. God's peace surpasses understanding. Isn't that what it means in Philippians 4:7 when it talks about a peace that transcends understanding? I know that God is using the very things in my life that caused me intense suffering to bring incredible comfort. When I sing, when I speak, His healing virtue is pouring through my wounds. Even now in the places where I am still broken, God shines His glory through my holes.

He'll use us in our weakness, and we will see His strength. We don't have to be perfect to shine His life, we just have to live with abandonment and make ourselves available to Him. And besides, people aren't asking us to be perfect; they are asking us to be real.

When we look at the healing virtue of Jesus, we can see that it didn't come from His risen body or the empty tomb. It came from His wounds. It came at the cross.

AND THE PEACE OF *God,* WHICH SURPASSES
ALL UNDERSTANDING, WILL *Guard* YOUR HEARTS
AND MINDS THROUGH CHRIST JESUS.

PHILIPPIANS 4:7

So that You May Know...

So many times the Lord will do things or allow things to happen to us, just to show us that He is God.

I will give you the treasures of darkness,

riches stored in secret places,

so that you may know that I am the LORD.

Isaiah 45:3 (NIV)

THE WAY *to* HOPE

*W*e lose our way. We want hope. We want forgiveness. We want restoration. We want freedom.

We must continually take trips to the cross. We must live a life of repentance. We must keep our hands open so that God can fill them. He will forgive. He will restore. He will set free. We can be different than what life "sets us up to be."

Hebrews 10:22 says:

"*... let us draw near to God with a true heart in full assurance of faith, having our hearts sprinkled from an evil conscience and our bodies washed with pure water.*"

God's worthiness flows into our unworthiness and we become worthy. If we want the Lord to empower us, we must come under His rule. His commands are for us and not against us. They are not to constrain us, but to free us.

A LIFE OF HOPE

We must not miss the life God has for us. A life marked by His blessings. A life marked with supernatural provision. A life that is lived by Divine leading.

This is one of my favorite psalms:

I will exalt You, O LORD
for You lifted me out of the depths
and did not let my enemies gloat over me.
O LORD my God, I called to You for help
and You healed me.
O LORD, You brought me up from the grave;
you spared me from going down into the pit.
Sing to the LORD, You saints of His;
praise His holy name.
For His anger lasts only a moment,
but His favor lasts a lifetime;
weeping may remain for the night,
but rejoicing comes in the morning.
You turned my wailing into dancing;
You removed my sackcloth and clothed me with joy.
that my heart may sing to You and not be silent.
O LORD my God, I will give You thanks forever.

PSALM 30:1-5, 11 (NIV)

HE IS STILL GOD

It will get treacherous and dark. It will feel like a never—ending night.

But the morning will come.

The sun will rise again.

It will be a new day.

You will possess a new hope.

And you will see and receive new mercies.

Jesus Christ is not a security *from* storms. He is perfect security *in* storms.

Yes ... He is still God.

IF I TRUST IN GOD AND LOOK TO HIM—
WILL LIFE BE WONDERFUL?
THAT'S NOT THE QUESTION.
IS HE SOVEREIGN?
IS HE FAITHFUL?
ARE HIS PROMISES TRUE?
A RESOUNDING *YES*.

A Song

I'VE KNOWN LAUGHTER

DAYS OF FUN

HAD MANY HOURS IN THE SUN

BEEN TO MANY MOUNTAINS

WALKED ALONG THE OCEAN SHORES

I'VE SEEN RAINBOWS FILL THE SKY

COUNTED STARS ON SUMMER NIGHTS

OH, SO MANY MOMENTS

THAT HAVE FILLED MY SOUL WITH JOY

BUT, IT'S BEEN THE RAIN

IT'S BEEN THE STORMS

IT'S BEEN THE DAYS

WHEN I'VE BEEN WORN

THAT I HAVE FOUND YOU, LORD

THAT I HAVE SEEN YOU, FATHER

IT'S IN THE PAIN

THAT I HAVE GROWN

THROUGH ALL THE SORROW

I HAVE KNOWN

BUT, IF THAT'S WHAT IT TAKES

FOR YOU TO LEAD ME THIS FAR

GO AHEAD AND BREAK MY HEART.

"BREAK MY HEART" BY KATHY TROCCOLI